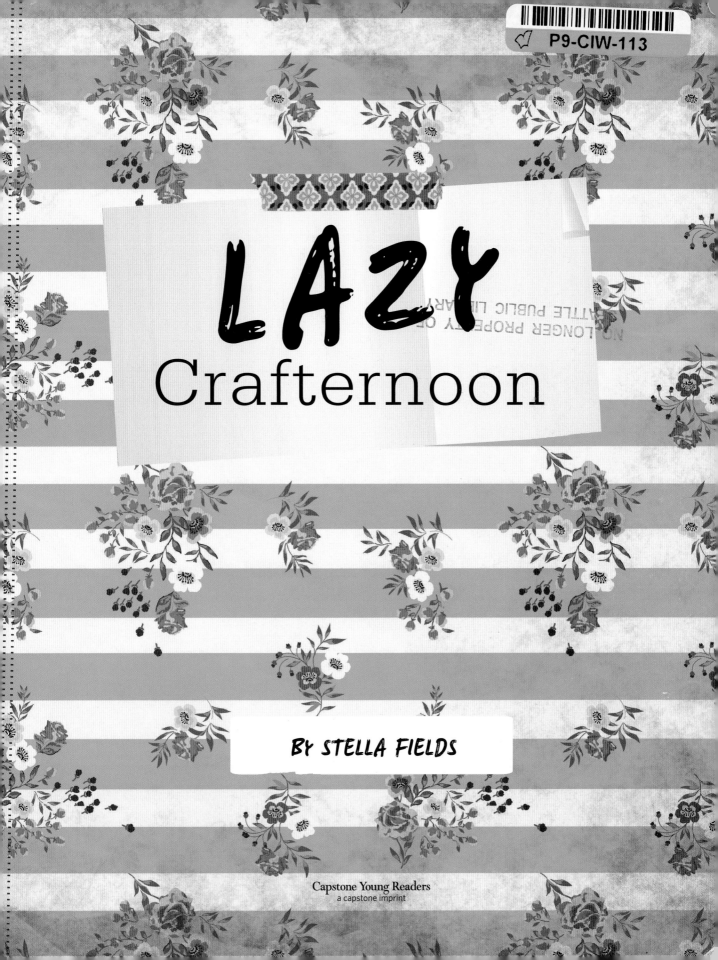

LAZY
Crafternoon

By STELLA FIELDS

Capstone Young Readers
a capstone imprint

CONTENTS

WHAT'S A LAZY CRAFTERNOON?

It's a day you spend with your friends, each of you making something incredible.

Doesn't sound lazy, right? But it can feel like it, especially with the fun, pretty projects in this book.

The crafts in this book are made for beginners, but they can be taken to a new level by crafters with more experience. The projects are organized by type — accessories you can wear, things to decorate your room or home, crafts to brighten up your school supplies and electronics, and projects that are perfect for planning parties.

These projects can be done on your own — nothing requires more than one person — but it's always more fun to spend a lazy crafternoon making things with your friends.

With some craft supplies, chill music, decadent snacks, and your best friends, any afternoon can be a lazy crafternoon.

HOST A LAZY CRAFTERNOON

To host a lazy crafternoon of your own, you only need four things: your friends, supplies, space, and snacks.

Start with your **friends.** Invite girls who already craft on their own, but don't stop there. Your fashionista friend already has a great sense for fabric. Your musician friend knows how to put things together. Your movie-loving friend has an eye for what looks great.

You'll need plenty of **supplies.** You can choose a few projects from this book and stock the supplies yourself, or just ask your friends to bring what they have. Many of the projects here use things you already have around the house. Check out pages 8-17 for some supplies that are used frequently in this book.

Before your friends arrive, get everything set up in your crafting **space.** You can craft on your bedroom floor or outside, but you might want to find a table where you can lay out the supplies and have room for everyone to work.

Snacks on sticks or cut into small, bite-sized pieces are great choices for people who don't want to get their hands dirty mid-craft. Some perfect recipes — with matching crafts — are on pages 112-127.

That's it! Now get lazy.

SUPPLIES

There's nothing worse than trying to make something and realizing you don't have everything you need. Each project in this book has a list of necessary supplies. You will also need basic crafting tools such as paintbrushes, scissors, and glue. But don't worry: most of the supplies you need to make the projects in *Lazy Crafternoon* are less than $10, and all of them are easy to find at craft stores, hardware stores, online, and even at some department stores.

DECOUPAGE GLUE

Decoupage glue is an acrylic, non-toxic, water-based liquid that works as both a glue and a sealer. Some varieties have a special varnish added to give them a matte or glossy finish. Because it is water-based, decoupage can easily be wiped or sponged away. It's easy for beginners to use, and more experienced crafters will find ways to turn this simple medium into true masterpieces.

You can add as many layers of decoupage as you want to your project. Create works of art that are multidimensional. Paint over decoupage with acrylic paint. Spray with sealant and then write over the top with permanent marker.

HOW TO USE IT: Before you glue, prep your supplies. Test your prepped work surface by decoupaging a small piece of fabric or paper onto it. Let the decoupage dry completely. If the fabric or paper peels right off, your project probably won't work.

WHERE TO FIND IT: Any craft store

COST: Less than $10 for a jar that'll last through quite a few projects

WASHI TAPE

If you've wandered through a craft store recently, you've probably seen rolls of colorful tape taking over the shelves. For those who haven't, washi tape is a craft tape similar to masking tape that is colorful, easy to tear, and repositionable. It is made with thin paper that makes the tape appear translucent.

Traditional Japanese washi uses paper made from natural fibers such as bamboo, rice, or hemp. However, other companies around the world have produced their own versions. Similar varieties, such as fabric tape, glitter tape, tissue tape, and paper tape are included in this book. Different brands vary in quality and consistency; shop around and find the brands that work best for you and your projects.

HOW TO USE IT: Just like tape, stick it to your project and cut any excess.

WHERE TO FIND IT: Any craft store; you can also get it online or at many department stores.

COST: Around $5 for a roll, though you can find some that's cheaper and some that's more expensive.

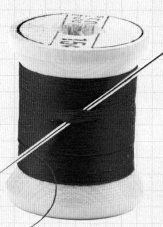

NEEDLE & THREAD

If you or one of your friends have (and know how to use) a sewing machine, that's the best way to handle most of the sewing projects in this book. But if not, don't fret—there are other options!

HOW TO USE IT: To sew by hand, slide the thread through the eye of the needle. Tie the end of the thread into a knot. Poke the needle through the underside of the fabric. Pull the thread through the fabric to the knotted end. Poke your needle back through the fabric and up again to make a stitch.

Continue weaving the needle in and out of the fabric, making small stitches in a straight line. When you are finished sewing, make a loose stitch. Thread the needle through the loop and pull tight. Cut off remaining thread.

WHERE TO FIND IT: Any craft store and many department stores

COST: You can buy a pack of needles and some thread for less than $5.

OTHER SUPPLIES

acrylic paint
adhesive letters
beads
canvases
cardstock
chalkboard paint
clay pot
clear phone case
circle punch
craft foam
craft knife
d-ring

industrial glue
markers
metal clips
needle and thread
oil-based markers
paintbrushes
paper lantern
plastic bangle bracelet
polymer clay

decoupage glue
embroidery floss
embroidery hoop
fabric
fabric glue
fabric paint
freezer paper
glitter
glue sticks
hole punch
hot glue and hot glue gun

ribbon
rotary cutter and mat
sandpaper
scrapbook paper
sewing machine
stamps and stamp pads
thread
tissue paper
toothpicks
T-shirts
washi tape
wire
wooden birdhouse
yarn

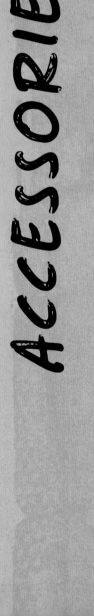

ACCESSORIES

A pretty phone case unlike anyone else's—personalize your phone in a snap.

WASHI PHONE CASE

1. Trace the cell phone cover onto the tagboard. Be sure to include camera and microphone holes.

2. Cut out the tracing. Use the craft knife to cut out the camera and microphone holes.

3. Decorate the tagboard with tape. Try using various angles and lengths of tape. Washi and glitter tape can be layered, woven, cut, and adjusted as desired.

4. Place the tagboard tracing inside the cell phone cover, and insert the phone.

The great thing about this project is that you'll have plenty of supplies for multiple inserts. You can use a different one every day or swap them out whenever you want to. Make matching ones with your friends or use similar tape so your cases coordinate.

BRAIDED NECKLACE

Dress up a plain T-shirt with this perfect accessory.

2

3

4

5

6

WHAT YOU'LL NEED

fabric scraps
rubber band
ribbon (about 1 inch (2.5 cm) wide
    and 12 inches (30 cm) long)
needle and thread

1 Cut or tear your fabric into 1-inch-wide (2.5 cm) lengths. Make three pieces about 18 inches (46 cm) long, three pieces that are 15 inches (38 cm) long, and three pieces that are 12 inches (30 cm) long.

2 Use a rubber band to put the three 18-inch-long pieces together.

3 Braid the fabric pieces together. Use a rubber band to keep together at the end.

4 Repeat steps 1-3 twice more with the other lengths.

5 Sew the end of each braid to keep it from unravelling.

6 Hold one end from each braid together and sew a piece of ribbon over the top of the braid. Do the same on the other side with the other end of the ribbon. Cut off any extra fabric.

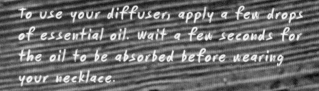

To use your diffuser, apply a few drops of essential oil. Wait a few seconds for the oil to be absorbed before wearing your necklace.

DIFFUSER NECKLACES

A mood-uplifter you can wear (and it's so pretty, too)!

WHAT YOU'LL NEED

polymer clay
bottle cap
stamp
toothpick
beads
hemp thread

1 Knead the polymer clay with your hands until it's soft and pliable.

2 Pat or roll the clay out on your work surface until the clay is about 0.25 inch (0.6 cm) thick.

3 Use the bottle cap like a cookie cutter to cut out clay circles.

4 Decorate the clay circles with the stamp.

5 Make a hole near the top of each circle with the toothpick.

6 Set the clay circles on a baking sheet and bake according to the directions on the clay package. Let cool completely.

7 Cut a length of hemp thread about 24 inches (61 cm) long. Fold it in half and push the folded piece through the hole. Push the cut ends through the loop and pull the loop tight. Add one or two beads, knotting the thread after each bead, and knot the top to close.

Try some of these essential oils, alone or in combination:

HEADACHES: *peppermint, frankincense, lavender*
SLEEP: *chamomile, lavender*
ENERGY: *peppermint, frankincense, lemon*
RELAXATION: *lavender, sandalwood, bergamot*
MEMORY: *rosemary, lemon*
MOOD: *lavender, lemon*

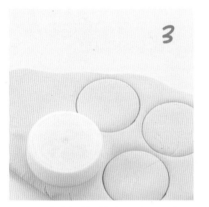

3

4

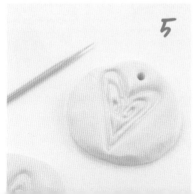

5

All you need to make these adorable headbands is fabric, a needle, and thread.

FABRIC HEADBANDS TWO WAYS

TIED BOW HEADBAND

WHAT YOU'LL NEED

one or two fabric pieces
22 inches (56 cm) long
and 6 inches (15 cm) wide
bottle cap

 1 Measure and cut a piece of fabric about 6 inches (15 cm) wide by 22 inches (56 cm) long.

2 Fold the strip in half (with right sides together). Use a bottle cap to trace a half circle on both ends of the fabric.

 3 Sew along one half circle and halfway down the long side of the fabric. Leave a 3-inch (7.5 cm) space and continue sewing down the long side of the fabric and the curve on the other end.

4 Trim off the extra fabric on the curves. Then flip right side out through the space in the seam.

5 Sew opening closed.

6 Wrap headband around head and tie with a double knot.

INFINITY HEADBAND

 1 Cut two strips of fabric, each 6 inches wide (15 cm) and 22 inches (56 cm) long.

2 Fold each strip in half (with right sides facing) and sew down the long side of raw edges, forming two tubes.

3 Flip the tubes right side out and lay them down, seam side up, in the shape of an X. Fold strips over so that they are linked together, matching up the raw edges.

 Sewing tip: The right side of the fabric is the printed side. The other side is called the wrong side.

4 Take unfinished headband and wrap around head, adjusting for proper fit. Then line up all raw edges and sew together. Cut off any excess.

Pretty headphones that
stand out in a crowd.

WRAPPED
HEADPHONES

WHAT YOU'LL NEED

earbud headphones
toothpick
nail polish in one to three colors
clear topcoat nail polish
embroidery floss in three colors

1 If using old earbuds, clean gently with soap and warm water.

2 Use the colored nail polish and toothpick to paint the earbuds and the headphone jack. Avoid painting anything metal or any parts that go in your ear. Also do not paint over any holes. When the nail polish is dry, use the clear topcoat to cover.

3 Cut the embroidery floss to about four times the length of the headphones cord.

4 Tie the floss to the plug end of the headphones. Hold down the ends and start wrapping.

5 Wrap until you reach the end. To finish, just tie a knot and trim the edges.

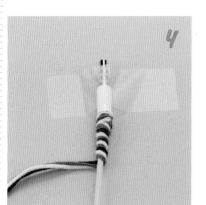

You'll want to wear these sunglasses even when it's cloudy.

DECOUPAGE SUNGLASSES

WHAT YOU'LL NEED:

eyeglass kit or small screwdriver
sunglasses
scrapbook paper
satin decoupage glue and foam brush
dimensional decoupage glue

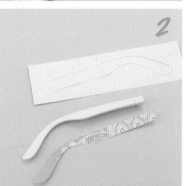

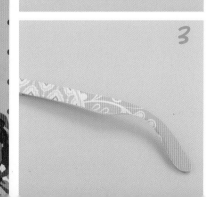

1 Use the screwdriver to remove the sunglasses' temples (the part that goes over your ear). Set the lenses and screws aside.

2 Trace the temples onto the scrapbook paper. Cut out and trim, if necessary.

3 Brush a thin layer of satin decoupage glue onto the outside of the temples. Stick the paper cutouts to them. Press out any creases or bubbles with your fingers. Let dry completely.

4 Place temples paper-side-up on a newspaper-lined work surface. Starting at one end, cover the scrapbook paper with dimensional glue. Use a rag to catch any glue drips. Let dry completely. Repeat with the other sides of the temples.

5 Reattach the temples to the glasses' frame.

BEAD AND HEMP BRACELETS

sweet bracelets for the fashionista.

1 Decide how long you would like your bracelet. Add one inch, and then double the length. Cut the leather cording to that length.

2 Thread your needle on a 12-inch (30 cm) piece of thread. Tie a knot in the end of the threads.

3 Thread all the beads onto the thread. Tie a knot at the end to secure, leaving a 1-inch (2.5 cm) tail. Cut off any excess thread.

4 Fold leather cording and tie the thread to the leather, creating a small leather loop.

5 Cut a 10-foot (3 m) piece of hemp cord and begin wrapping the hemp cord at the base of the leather loop. Be sure to tuck the hemp cord tail in while wrapping. Wrap your hemp cord until you reach your first bead.

6 Wrap the hemp cord between each bead once from left to right. When you get to the bottom of the bracelet, create a loop in the leather cord and then wrap the hemp cord around the bracelet a few times.

7 Wrap the hemp cord back up the bracelet from right to left. When you reach your last bead, create another leather loop by tucking the end under the hemp wrapping. Cut off any excess hemp cord.

8 Attach a jump ring to each leather loop, and then attach toggle clasp to jump rings.

Stay cozy and warm in this gorgeous infinity scarf.

INFINITY SCARF

WHAT YOU'LL NEED

two pieces of fabric, each 14 inches
   (35.5 cm) wide and 72 inches
   (1.8 m) long. The fabric can be the
   same for both pieces, or they can be
   coordinating prints.
needle and thread
buttons (optional)

1 Pin the right sides of the fabric pieces together. Then sew down each long side.

2 Flip right side out.

3 Sew the short ends together. Add buttons if you choose.

Try combining coordinating fabric!

This makes a quick and easy gift, especially if you're using a sewing machine.

DECOUPAGE SHOES

Guarantee you'll have the most original shoes by decoupaging your own pair!

1. Cut out pieces of fabric or paper in whatever shapes you want.

2. Decide where you want to place the pieces on the shoes. They can be uneven or mismatched—whatever you think looks best.

3. Cover the first shoe with a layer of decoupage.

4. Carefully place each piece of fabric or paper on the shoe. Make sure that the piece is flat on the shoe and there are no air bubbles.

5. Repeat with the second shoe.

6. Cover both shoes in decoupage at least three times to seal your work.

You can use an old comic book, magazine pages, heavyweight wrapping paper, scrapbooking paper, or fabric for this project. Your shoes will last longest if you keep them dry—no splashing in puddles!

GRAPHIC TEE

T-shirts from the mall are so boring. Make your own!

1 Draw your design onto a piece of paper. When you're happy with it, set the freezer paper on top, shiny-side-down, and trace the design onto the freezer paper.

2 Put the freezer paper onto a protected work surface. (A big piece of cardboard or a clipboard works well for this part.) Use the craft knife to cut out the design.

3 Place a piece of cardboard inside the T-shirt. (This keeps your paint from bleeding through.) Using a low setting, iron the freezer paper stencil onto the T-shirt. The stencil should feel secure and not move.

4 Paint over the stencil using the fabric paint. You may need several coats. Let the paint dry completely between coats.

5 When the paint is dry, use a low setting to iron the front of the shirt. Then peel off the stencil. When you wash your shirt, make sure to turn it inside out.

When cutting your stencil, keep in mind that the parts you're cutting out are the parts that will get painted. You'll either need to make sure it's all one piece, or keep track of any small pieces

You can reuse your pattern to make another shirt with the same print, but for best results, cut a new stencil for each shirt.

DECORATE

NO-SEW PILLOWS

Get cozy with this easy-to-make pillow. Make one or make a bunch—the more the cuddlier.

1 Lay fabric flat, right side down, on your work surface. Set the pillow on top of the fabric. Trace around the pillow, adding 2 inches (5 cm) on all sides.

2 Cut out the square. Repeat to make a second fabric square. Set the pillow aside.

3 Fold the edges of both fabric squares in about 1 inch (2.5 cm), and iron the creases flat.

4 Place fusible webbing tape along the edges of one fabric square. Set the second fabric square on top of the first, right side up so the creases line up. Iron three of the squares' sides together.

5 Push your pillow into the cover. Press the edge of the pillow down as you iron the last side closed.

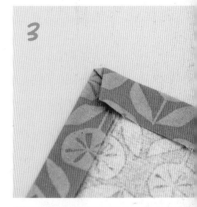

Fusible webbing tape works like sewing without sewing—the iron bonds the tape to fabric. It's usually less than $5 for a roll that's about 30 feet (10 meters) long. You can also use it to hem too-long clothes or curtains.

A gorgeous way to add some color to your windows—
or even a plain wall. You can draw a picture or create
a pattern—whatever matches your decor.

FAUX STAINED GLASS

1. Take the photo frame apart. Discard the backing and any paper inserts. Clean the frame's glass with rubbing alcohol, if necessary.

2. Decorate the window glass with permanent markers. Create your own design or trace a favorite design by placing it under the glass.

3. Cover the ink with a layer of decoupage. Let dry completely, and then repeat, coloring each section again and making sure to add decoupage after each layer. The more layers of marker, the deeper the finished colors will be.

4. Outline the edges of your design with black or metallic markers to really make your design stand out.

5. Use glue to attach the glass to the photo frame.

Not feeling creative? You can use this technique to display a favorite quote or poem. Write the words in one color and draw around them in another, or write each word in a different color.

PERFECT LAMPSHADE

Upgrade a lampshade with fresh fabric!

Try matching your desk lamp to a larger floor lamp with the same fabric, or cover two same-size lamps with coordinating fabrics for a richer look.

Make sure your fabric isn't too dark—paler colors let the light through better!

1   With the fabric right-side down, trace the top and bottom of your lampshade, leaving 1 inch (2.5 cm) between the shade and the line. To do this, you will roll your shade across the fabric, tracing as you do so, until you have completed a full circle and you are back at the beginning.

2   Cut fabric along the line, then wrap around the shade to make sure it fits properly.

3   Glue the fabric at the seam on one side. Continue gluing around the entire shade.

4   Glue down the extra fabric on the bottom and top. If your shade has small metal parts, cut a small slit in the fabric so it can easily go over the metal.

5   Trim off the extra fabric on the inside of the shade, or add ribbon for a more finished interior look.

6   Add ribbon or trim to the outside of the shade for the finishing touches.

PRETTY LIGHT SWITCH

why should the rest of your room have all the fun?

WHAT YOU'LL NEED

scrapbook paper
light switch plate
craft knife
stamp and stamp pad (optional)
matte decoupage glue
paintbrush

1   Lay the scrapbook paper face down on your work surface. Trace the light switch plate onto the paper and cut out.

2   (Optional) Use the stamp and stamp pad to decorate the scrapbook paper. Work in small sections. Continue stamping until the entire paper is decorated.

3   Use the decoupage glue to attach the scrapbook paper to the light switch plate.

You can use the same technique with outlet covers. Of course, you'll need an adult to detach and reattach them; you don't want to mess with electricity!

PAPER SCRAP CANVAS

Get scrap happy! Put out a pile of paper for everyone to use. Then set up work stations with canvases and decoupage glue.

1. Cut scrapbook paper into 1- by 3-inch (2.5-7.5cm) strips.

2. Arrange strips into a zigzag pattern on the canvas, plotting out the order from strip to strip. Leave a little white space between each strip. You'll have to trim some of your pieces to make them fit.

3. Apply decoupage on the back of each strip and place on canvas. It works best to start on one side and work your way to the other, making sure the space between each strip stays even.

4. When your pattern is complete, apply a layer of decoupage over the entire canvas. Let it dry, and then add another layer.

5. Wrap a ribbon around the canvas or paint the outside edges to give it a clean look.

You can use this same technique with fabric instead of scrapbook paper—or mix your media with both.

GOLD CONFETTI CANVAS

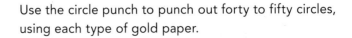

WHAT YOU'LL NEED

1-inch (2.5 cm) circle punch
two to three kinds of gold paper
canvas
spray adhesive or glue stick

1 Use the circle punch to punch out forty to fifty circles, using each type of gold paper.

2 Glue the circles onto the canvas in a scattered, free-form way.

MESSAGE CANVAS

WHAT YOU'LL NEED

painter's tape
white paint
canvas
colored paint
pencil
black fabric marker

1. Tape horizontal stripes across the entire canvas, leaving equal spaces between. Brush the edges of each piece of tape with white paint and let dry. Then paint over the entire canvas with your colored paint.

2. Allow paint to dry and remove tape slowly. Touch up any imperfections with colored paint and a small brush.

3. Once painted stripes are completely dry, lightly pencil a word or phrase on the canvas. Color in with black fabric marker.

Whether it's on your front door, bedroom door, or a wall, this wreath is bright and beautiful.

RIBBON WREATH

WHAT YOU'LL NEED

rotary cutter and cutting mat
ribbon, fabric, and tulle in a
variety of colors and patterns
wire wreath frame

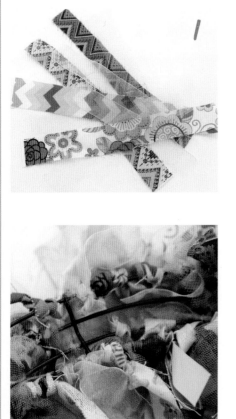

1 Use the rotary cutter to cut ribbon, fabric, and tulle into pieces about 8 inches (20 cm) long and 1 to 2 inches (2.5-5 cm) wide.

2 Start tying your pieces to the inside of the wreath frame. Begin with the innermost ring. Use a double knot to make sure the pieces stay on.

3 Continue tying around the wreath, bunching the fabrics together if desired.

4 Be sure to cover at least the inner and outer rings of the wreath. Depending how how thick you want your wreath, you may not want or need to use all the rings.

Use at least half a dozen different ribbons, fabric, and tulle for visual interest. Don't stop there, though. Use as many colors and patterns as you want.

You will need a lot of materials for your wreath. Buy more than you think you will need, so you don't come up short!

FLOWERPOTS THREE WAYS

Fresh flowers and growing green plants brighten anyone's day. Dress up simple flower pots by using one (or all!) of these techniques.

DECOUPAGE FLOWERPOT

WHAT YOU'LL NEED

sandpaper
clay pot
outdoor acrylic paint (optional)
assortment of fabric scaps
outdoor decoupage glue
acrylic sealer

1 Use the sandpaper to make the surface of the pot rough. This helps paint and glue adhere.

2 Paint top rim of pot (inside and out), if you like.

3 While paint is drying, cut fabric into small shapes and strips.

4 Brush each fabric piece with decoupage and glue onto pot. Cover the pot with fabric pieces until all of the clay is covered and you are pleased with your fabric design.

5 Cover the pot with decoupage, letting it dry between coats. Once dry, cover with acrylic sealer.

GOLD PAINTED FLOWERPOT

WHAT YOU'LL NEED

sandpaper
clay pot with saucer
acrylic paint (any color)
painter's tape
gold acrylic paint
acrylic sealer

1 Sand pot.

2 Paint the pot in a color of your choice.

3 Once the paint dries, tape off a section of the flower pot with painter's tape. Use the gold acrylic paint inside the painter's tape lines. Remove the tape.

4 After paint has dried, cover pot with acrylic sealer.

CHALKBOARD FLOWERPOT

WHAT YOU'LL NEED

sandpaper
clay pot
acrylic paints
stencil
chalkboard paint
chalk

1 Sand pot.

2 Paint the rim of the pot in a solid color and allow to dry. You may need to apply a second coat depending on the color.

3 Use a stencil and small paintbrush to design a pattern on the rim of the pot. You can also leave the rim a solid color or freehand draw a pattern.

4 Turn the pot upside down and apply the chalkboard paint to the remainder of the pot.

5 Apply a second coat of chalkboard paint and allow to dry twenty-four hours. Use chalk to write on the paint!

These sweet little houses look great together or by themselves.

BIRDHOUSES THREE WAYS

This craft is all about turning a zero into a hero!

PAINT CHIP BIRDHOUSE

WHAT YOU'LL NEED

acrylic paint
wood birdhouse
circle punch
paint chips
decoupage glue

1. Paint the birdhouse and let dry.

2. Use a circle craft punch to cut circles from paint chips.

3. Starting at the bottom of the birdhouse, brush a layer of decoupage onto the birdhouse. Position the paint chip circles on the decoupage, smoothing out from the center with your fingers. Alternate colors and tones on each row.

4. Apply more decoupage over the paper. Repeat for each section. Let dry. Trim the edges, if necessary.

5. To create scallops, let the circles hang halfway over the row below. Use a craft knife to cut out the shapes for the perches and holes.

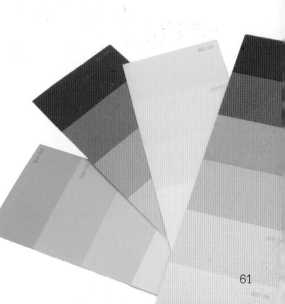

DECOUPAGE BIRDHOUSE

1 Paint the edges of the birdhouse that won't be covered by papers.

2 Cut the scrapbook paper to fit each section.

3 Brush decoupage on one section of the birdhouse at a time. Position the scrapbook paper on the section, smoothing out from the center with your fingers. Apply more decoupage over the paper.

4 Repeat for each section. Let dry. Trim the edges, if necessary. Add your own paintings or drawings to personalize your paper selections!

WHAT YOU'LL NEED

acrylic paint
wood birdhouse
scrapbook paper
decoupage glue

FABRIC-COVERED BIRDHOUSE

1. Paint birdhouse roof a solid color.

2. Cut fabrics to fit each section of the birdhouse.

3. Brush decoupage on one section of the birdhouse at a time. Position the fabric on the section, smoothing out from the center with fingers. Apply more decoupage over the fabric.

4. Repeat step 3 for each section. Let dry.

5. Add ribbon trim along the edges.

6. Create roof adornments by covering wooden shapes with fabrics. Hot glue the shapes to the roof.

WHAT YOU'LL NEED

acrylic paint
wood birdhouse
fabric scraps
decoupage glue
ribbon
wooden shapes
hot glue and hot glue gun

SCHOOL SUPPLIES

FANCY PENCILS

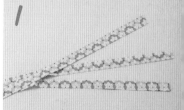

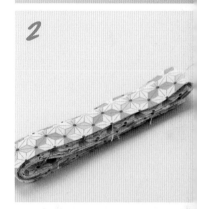

1 Cut fabric into strips that are about 24 inches (60 cm) long and ½ inch (1.2 cm) wide.

2 Fold a strip in half, and then keep folding until your strip is about 3 inches (7.5 cm) long.

3 Tie the fabric in the middle. Then cut the folded ends.

4 Fluff up the fabric to make a pom-pom.

5 Cover your pencil in white glue. Wrap a piece of fabric around and down the length of the pencil.

6 Use hot glue or small headpins to attach the pom-poms to the ends of the pencils.

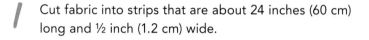

Before you sharpen these pencils, pull the fabric away and cut off the amount you'll sharpen.

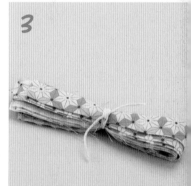

YARN-WRAPPED JARS

Perfect for storing pencils, holding flowers, or just on display by themselves, these jars make perfect gifts for anyone who wants to brighten up their room.

1 Use hot glue to attach a yarn strand near the top of the bottle.

2 Starting at the top of the jar or bottle, cover a section with white glue, and then wrap the yarn over the glued portion. Make sure the loops of yarn are tight and as close together as possible. Continue wrapping and gluing.

3 If you want to change colors, just snip the yarn and secure the loose end with more hot glue. Then continue wrapping and gluing with a new color of yarn.

4 When you reach the bottom of the jar, cut the yarn and use hot glue to seal the end.

You can yarn-wrap more than just bottles! Wooden letters, flower pots, wreaths, and even furniture (think chair legs) are all easy to wrap.

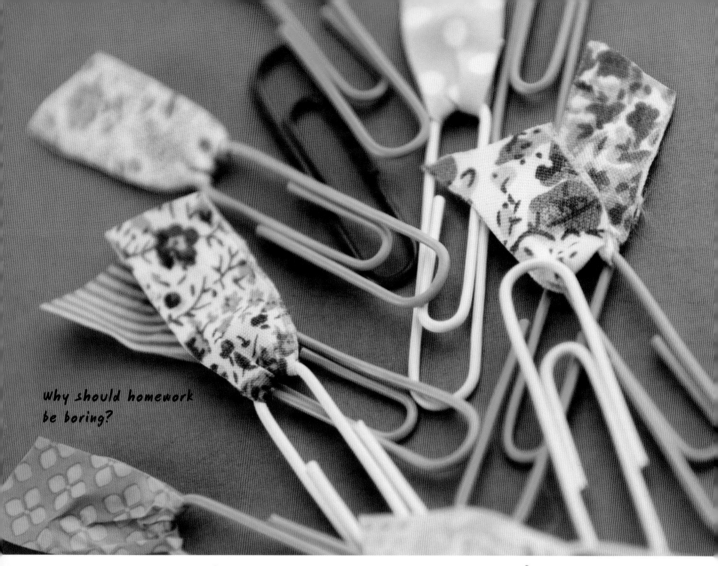

Why should homework be boring?

WASHI TAPE SCHOOL SUPPLIES

PAPER CLIPS

1. Simply loop washi tape around paper clip and trim the edge.

WHAT YOU'LL NEED

- paper clips
- pencils
- washi tape
- wax paper
- paper punch
- notebook

PENCILS

1 Cut a strip of washi tape that is the same length as a pencil.

2 Stick the cut strip onto the pencil and carefully wrap it, making sure there are no air bubbles.

3 Repeat with a second strip to completely cover.

These are quick to make, so make extras—your friends will want their own.

NOTEBOOK STICKERS

1 Place a strip of washi tape on wax paper.

2 Use a paper punch to cut the sticker design out of the washi tape and wax paper.

3 Peel the washi tape sticker off of the wax paper backing and place it onto a notebook.

Decorate your desk
with these pretty
paperweights.

PAINTED ROCKS

WHAT YOU'LL NEED

smooth round rocks
outdoor acrylic paints
painting pens
protective lacquer

1 Clean your rocks with warm water and let dry.

2 Choose your pattern or art and begin painting. You can use paint to cover the rock completely, or use painting pens for small details, or both!

3 Once your painted rock is dry, apply a layer of clear decoupage or protective lacquer. Let it dry and add one more layer.

Try writing short phrases or words on your rocks for little uplifters.

COLORFUL COMPUTER

You're not a plain Jane, and your computer doesn't have to be either.

WHAT YOU'LL NEED

washi tape
keyboard
laptop computer

1. For the keyboard: cut washi tape to fit the keys.

2. For the laptop: Cut fourteen strips of washi tape, each about 15 inches (38 cm) long. Lay seven of them down on your laptop lid, diagonally from top left to bottom right. Don't stick them down hard—just place them there.

3. Place one strip so that it is perpendicular to the strips you've already put down. Working one strip at a time, weave it over and under the other strips. Continue with the other six strips.

4. Trim the edges of the tape.

Leave some keys uncovered—or use clear washi tape—for maximum effect (and so you know where your fingers are supposed to go).

RIBBON ORGANIZER

Assignments, photos, notes, memorabilia—save it all in this pretty organizer.

WHAT YOU'LL NEED

large photo frame

spray paint

thumbtacks

fabric (2 inches (5 cm) larger on each side than the photo frame)

glue gun and hot glue

scissors

9-foot-long (3 m) piece of ½-inch- (1.2 cm) wide ribbon

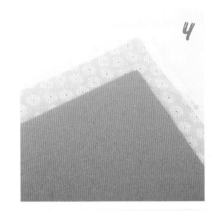

4

5

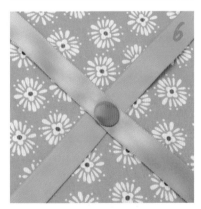

6

8

1 Take the photo frame apart. Set the cardboard backing aside, and discard the glass.

2 Set the frame on a protected work surface in a well-ventilated area. Color the frame with spray paint. Let the paint dry and repeat with a second coat, if desired. Set aside.

3 Repeat with the thumbtacks.

4 Lay the fabric pattern-side-down. Lay the cardboard over the fabric. Wrap the edges of the fabric tightly around the back of the cardboard. Hot glue the fabric edges to the backside of the cardboard.

5 Cut the ribbon into two 26-inch (66 cm) strips and four 13-inch (33 cm) strips. Arrange the strips in a crisscross pattern on the front of the bulletin board.

6 Use thumbtacks to hold the ribbons in place where they cross.

7 Turn the board over. Pull the end of one ribbon tight to the back of the board and hot glue in place. Repeat with both ends of all ribbons.

8 Reassemble photo frame.

PERSONALIZED NOTEBOOKS

Whether you're taking notes in class or keeping a journal, you'll love having these bright books to work in.

DECOUPAGE

1. Paint a thin layer of decoupage on front cover of the notebook.

2. Place scrapbook paper over notebook cover. Press down firmly to remove any unwanted air bubbles.

3. Flip notebook to inside front cover and fold over excess scrapbook paper on each side. Cut several slits in each corner to allow fold to contour corner if rounded.

4. Apply decoupage to folded-over paper and corners.

5. Flip notebook over and repeat steps 1-4 on back cover.

6. Wrap the spine of your notebook with several strips of washi tape, starting in the middle and working toward the top and bottom of the notebook. Wrap the extra tape onto the inside and trim to fit.

7. Decorate with inspirational stickers, letters, pictures, etc. using decoupage.

WHAT YOU'LL NEED

notebook
scrapbook paper
alphabet stickers
inspirational stickers
magazines
washi tape
decoupage
scissors

WASHI

1. Wrap the notebook horizontally with strips of washi tape.

2. Wrap the binding vertically.

3. Trim the edges of the washi tape.

QUICK FABRIC TOTE

WHAT YOU'LL NEED

two 14 by 16 inch (35 by 40 cm) pieces
   of cotton fabric
pins
two 23 ½ inch (60 cm) pieces of
   cotton webbing

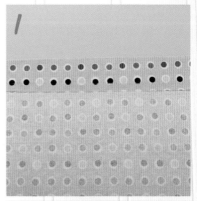

1   Lay one piece of fabric wrong-side-down. Fold the top edge in 1.5 inches (4 cm). Iron the fold.

2   Pin the handles onto the fold.

3   Sew along the top and bottom of the fold. Make sure to sew the handles down as well.

4   Repeat steps 1-3 with the second pieces of fabric and webbing.

5   Pin the bag halves together, right sides in. Snip the bottom corners off; this will help the bag look more finished.

6   Sew ½ inch (1.2 cm) from the edges to join the halves together. Use a backstitch when you get to both ends of the seam.

7   Use a zigzag stitch along the very edges of the bag. This will prevent the fabric edges from fraying.

8   Turn the bag right side out. It's ready to use!

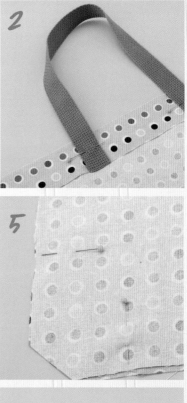

Carry your books in style!

DIY TABLET COVER

WHAT YOU'LL NEED

sheet of foam

½ yard (.5 m) of fabric

iron

¼-inch-wide (.6 cm) elastic ribbon

button

needle and thread (or sewing machine)

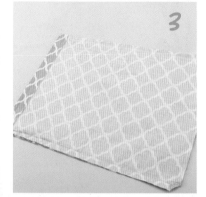

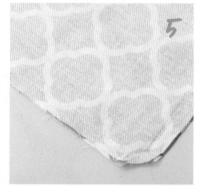

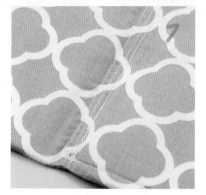

1   Trace and cut out your tablet's shape onto the foam. Repeat for a second piece.

2   Set the foam shapes onto the fabric. Leave ½ inch (1.3 cm) between the pieces of foam. Trace ½ inch around the outside of the foam. Add an extra inch on the left side of the foam. Cut out the fabric piece. Repeat to make a second piece.

3   Fold the left edges of the fabric pieces in one inch, and iron in place.

4   Place the fabric pieces on top of each other, wrong sides out. Sew along the top, bottom, and right sides of the fabric, leaving ¼-inch (.6cm) for a seam allowance.

5   Trim the corners of the seams for a clean fold. Then turn the cover inside out, so the bright sides of the fabric are out.

6   Slip the foam pieces into the fabric case. Leave ½ inch (1.2 cm) between the pieces.

7   Pin the left edges of the fabric together, and sew closed. Sew three lines of stitches up the center of the cover to create a spine.

8   Set the tablet on the right side of the cover. Pin elastic in all four corners. When it's placed how you want, sew the elastic in place.

9   Sew a button to the front of the cover. Sew a loop of elastic to the back of the cover, to keep the cover closed.

You can make this for any brand of tablet. It's way more fun than going to a store and buying a boring plain cover.

Don't just hide your special stuff in shoeboxes. These pretty fabric boxes bring a splash of color.

FABRIC-COVERED BOXES

1 Place the fabric right side down on your work surface. Set the box in the center of the fabric and trace around the edges. Don't cut on this line—you'll need it later.

2 Measure and cut the fabric to the height of the box, plus one inch. You're wrapping the entire box, so make sure the fabric is wide enough to stretch from the top of one side along the bottom and to the top of the other side.

3 Pick up the box and apply fabric glue to the bottom. Set the box back onto the fabric, making sure it sits inside the lines you drew in step 1.

4 Make cut from the corner of the fabric square to the nearest box corner. Repeat with all four corners.

5 Fold one long side of the fabric up and tuck it inside the box. Use fabric glue to hold it in place. Repeat with the other long side.

6 Repeat step 5 with the short sides of the box.

7 Repeat steps 1-5 with the box's lid.

Two presents in one! Use one of these boxes as a perfect way to give a gift. No wrapping paper to throw away, and your giftee can use it for storage of her own.

CELEBRATE

RIBBON CHANDELIER

Every room needs
a chandelier. Bring
color and surprise to
your decor with this
simple project.

3

1. Cut ribbon to varying lengths, between 18-24 inches (45-60 cm) long. Tie each piece to the embroidery hoop.

2. Keep adding and trimming until the chandelier feels complete. Make sure to mix up your materials so the colors, textures, and designs are spread out.

3. Tie 3 18-inch-long (45 cm) pieces of ribbon to the hoop at equal distances around the circle. Knot them together, and hang from a hook.

These imperfect knots add to the fun of the chandelier!

Want more detail? Add pom-poms, bells, shells, and lace. After being used to decorate a party, this chandelier will look amazing in your room!

Nothing says "party time" like bunting! Hang this easy party banner around the room for an instant crafternoon feel. Fabric, sewing supplies, and bias tape are all you need to bring everything together.

FABRIC BUNTING

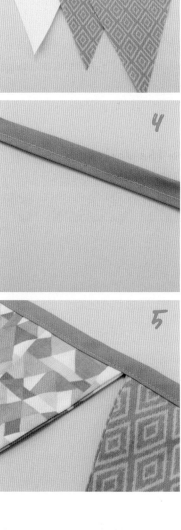

WHAT YOU'LL NEED

cardstock, ruler, and pencil
four different types of fabric,
 1 yard (.9 m) each
bias tape
sewing machine or hot glue gun
iron

1 Use a piece of cardstock and a ruler to make a triangle template. The triangle should be about 6.5 inches (16.5 cm) wide and 8.5 inches (21.5 cm) tall.

2 Trace the template onto the fabric and cut out your triangles. Each triangle piece needs a front and a back.

3 Stack each pair of triangle pieces with their right sides together and sew (or glue) along the long edges. Trim any stray threads, turn the triangles right side out, and iron them flat.

4 Sew (or glue) the first 6 to 8 inches (15 to 20 cm) of bias tape shut. Then open the tape and tuck the short end of a triangle between the folds. Sew (or glue) the bias tape shut, sandwiching the triangle inside. Continue adding triangles and sewing or gluing.

5 Once all the triangles are used up, sew (or glue) a 6 to 8 inch (15 to 20 cm) tail at the end of the bias tape. Your banner is now ready to hang!

You can use just a few different fabrics for a streamlined look, or choose dozens to use up leftovers and make a multi-colored bunting. Either way, it'll be gorgeous!

91

Bring some light to the dark with these delightful luminaries!

DECOUPAGE MASON JAR

WHAT YOU'LL NEED

tissue paper
mason jars
decoupage glue
ribbon or yarn
wire
beads
LED candle

1 Cut the tissue paper into wide strips or use a circle punch to punch out circles of tissue paper.

2 Brush decoupage onto the jar and press tissue paper down, making sure to eliminate any air bubbles. When the jar is covered, add a final coat of decoupage.

3 Glue ribbon or yarn to the top of jar.

4 If you like, add a wire handle by winding wire a few times around the top and making a large loop around the opening. Add beads for a finishing touch.

5 Place LED candles inside jars to illuminate.

These are gorgeous in sunlight, but they're even prettier at night, all lit up by the candles inside. Try different colors of tissue paper to create different illuminated effects.

The perfect party decoration, the tassel garland packs a ton of punch—and all you need is tissue paper!

DIY TASSEL GARLAND

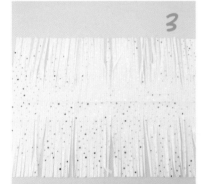

1   Take one piece of tissue paper. Lay it flat, and then fold in half widthwise. Fold in half lengthwise. Then fold again, lengthwise.

2   Place with the folded edge at the top. Make cuts ¼ inch apart (.6 cm) from the bottom up, leaving about an inch and a half at the top.

3   Unfold, and lay flat so that the fringe is horizontal. Untangle the fringe as necessary.

4   Starting at the bottom, roll up the paper. Once the entire sheet is rolled up, twist the center, tightly and gently.

5   Fold the two sides of tassel slices together. Twist the center around itself, creating a small loop in the top for a string.

6   Add a dot of hot glue to the loop to keep the tassel from untwisting.

Want a decoration in your room that you can change whenever you want? Buy a few different colors of tissue paper, and switch them out when you're bored.

Decorate these letters for any occasion.

PAPER DECOUPAGE LETTERS

WHAT YOU'LL NEED

paper mache letters
acrylic paint
scrapbook paper in several colors
   and patterns
craft knife
decoupage

1. Paint the sides of the letters with acrylic paint.

2. Flip the letters backward and trace onto scrapbook paper.

3. Using the craft knife, cut out the scrapbook letters.

4. Coat the letter with decoupage. Place the scrapbook paper on top of the cardboard letter, pressing out any air bubbles, and let it dry for a few minutes.

5. While the decoupage dries, cut out any additional shapes you want to add. Layer additional paper with decoupage.

6. When you're done, add another layer of decoupage to the top of the letters to seal the paper.

Spell out a birthday girl's name, or supply each guest's initial and let them decoupage it themselves.

You can use any paper to decoupage these letters— try comic book pages, pages from an old dictionary or book, etc.

Even your living room can feel like a summer garden with these pretty floral puffs.

HANGING FLOWER BALLS

2

3

4

5

1 Using a craft punch, cut scalloped circles from tissue paper. You'll need a lot of circles, so plan on punching them out for a while.

2 Stack 8 circles on top of each other. Staple the center of the circles.

3 Fluff the stapled tissue paper up to look like a flower.

4 Glue flowers to the paper lantern. Continue until lantern is completely covered.

5 Hang with a length of ribbon.

This is the perfect type of project to do while talking to your friends. It's pretty lazy, so your attention can be on your conversation, not so much on what your hands are doing. If you're alone, you could do this while watching a movie.

These balloons are extra special!

GLITTER BALLOONS

Add tissue paper tassels, made using the technique on page 94, for an even prettier decoration.

WHAT YOU'LL NEED

clear jumbo balloons
tissue paper
craft punch, confetti, or glitter
balloon pump
paper funnel

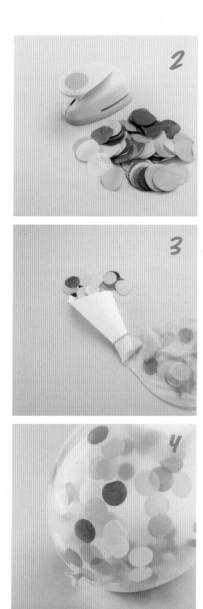

1 Use the craft punch to make confetti out of tissue paper.

2 Fill the balloon with your choice of tissue paper confetti, store-bought confetti, or glitter. A paper funnel can help make this easier.

3 Blow up the balloon and tie to close.

Could anything be lovelier than these gorgeous gift decorations?

PAPER FLOWER GIFT TOPPERS

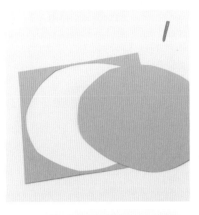

1

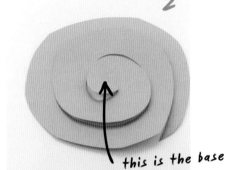

2

this is the base

3

4

1. Cut a 6 inch (15 cm) circle from a piece of paper.

2. Cut a spiral from your circle, starting from the outside edge working your way to the middle. As you approach the center of the circle, leave a larger middle area so there is a base. This will be used later for gluing the flower together.

3. Start rolling up the spiral from the outside all the way to the center. Keep it as tight as you can.

4. After rolling up about 1 or 2 inches (2.5-5 cm) of the spiral, add a small dot of hot glue to make sure it still has a nice tight center when you are finished.

5. Stand your tightly coiled spiral upright, using the center piece as a base for your flower, and then let it unravel a little. Add some hot glue to the base and gently lower the rolled flower petals onto the base. Hold until dry.

These make great gift toppers, but see what else you can use them for!

These gift tags are incredibly easy
to make and have so many uses!

WASHI TAPE GIFT TAGS

1 If you're using cardstock, cut it into gift tag shapes and punch a small hole on one end.

2 Use washi tape to decorate the gift tags. You can also use stickers, markers, or glitter. Or make your own stickers, using the technique on page 71.

3 Tie a piece of ribbon or cording through the hole.

Your presents will be so pretty, no one will want to open them!

WASHI GIFT WRAP

WHAT YOU'LL NEED

gift box
solid wrapping paper
clear tape
washi tape
tags, ribbon, and twine (optional)

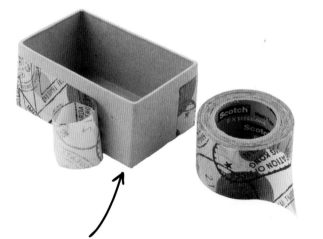

1 After boxing up your gift, wrap it in solid wrapping paper.

2 Wrap long strips of washi tape all the way around your box.

3 Add tags, ribbon, and twine.

Wrap your gift box in thicker washi tape for a different look!

You can't go wrong with this project. If you're wrapping a lot of gifts, do it in stages—wrap all of them first, then add washi tape to each package, and finally add the accents. This will keep your presents from looking alike!

Don't buy your cards at the store. Make them yourself for the perfect meaningful message.

DIY CARDS

STENCIL CARD

1 On the front of the card, stencil an animal, or something else you prefer.

2 Place four strips of washi tape, each slightly overlapping the next, below the animal.

HELLO CARD

1 On the front of the card, place three diagonal strips of washi tape. Leave a little space between the strips.

2 Use a burst and heart punch to cut out shapes. Glue to the card.

3 Use a computer to type *Hello* in a script. Print and cut, then attach to card.

THANK YOU CARD

1 Use a craft punch (or scissors) to cut the petals for the flower from one piece of scrapbook paper. Use another type of paper for the circle to make the middle of the flower. Glue onto the front of the card.

2 Use a computer to type *Thank You!* in a typewriter font. Print the page, and cut out the words. Glue beneath the flower. You can also write the words on paper.

DIY
ENVELOPES

1. Start with a square piece of paper with a corner pointing at you. Use a ruler to help you draw a light line between the corners of the paper to form an X. The center of the X is the center of the square. Fold the corners on the right and left into the center of the X.

2. Fold the bottom point so that the tip is about half an inch above the center of the X. Press the fold at the bottom down so it's a sharp crease. Add two strips of double-sided tape to hold the bottom flap in place.

3. Fold the top point down so it overlaps the center by half an inch. If you want to fasten the top flap in place, use double-sided tape or a sticker.

These are much easier than they look!

FOOD AND DRINK

SUNRISE SIPPER AND STAR CHARMS

This glittery mocktail is made even sweeter with a coordinating drink charm.

WHAT YOU'LL NEED

- colored sugar sprinkles
- edible glitter
- orange wedge
- grenadine or cherry juice
- orange juice
- pineapple juice
- 20g wire
- small star-shaped cookie cutter
- thin-gauge wire
- pliers
- beads

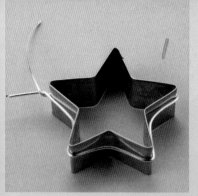

SUNRISE SIPPERS

1 Mix the sugar and edible glitter together on a small, shallow plate. Run the orange wedge around the edge of the glass, then turn the glass upside down to dip the lip in the sugar.

2 Flip the glass right side up. Pour a little grenadine into the bottom of the glass. Fill the glass two-thirds full with orange juice. Then add pineapple juice until the glass is full. Put the orange wedge on the edge of the glass as shown.

STAR CHARMS

1 Wrap a length of 20g wire around the contours of a small star-shaped cookie cutter. Use a small pliers to twist the two ends together.

2 Make a small loop with one end. Twist the wire below the loop twice, leaving a small tail of metal.

3 Twist the other end around the loop's tail, filling the small gap between the star and the loop. Cut off the extra wire.

4 Remove the wire star from the cookie cutter.

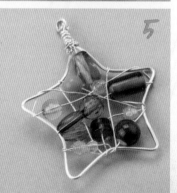

5 Cut a long length of thin-gauge wire. Secure one end of the wire to the star shape. Slide assorted beads onto the wire. Wrap the wire and beads around the star shape until you like how it looks. Then secure the end of the wire and cut off the excess. Set the star charm aside.

6 Cut a 2 inch (5 cm) length of wire. Wrap it around a small, round object (like a spool of thread). Make sure that the ends of the wire overlap about ½ inch (1.2 cm). Using a small pliers, turn one end of the wire into a loop, and bend the other end into a hook. Connect the two.

7 Slide the star charm onto the charm loop.

Even the sweetest of cakes can be made sweeter with this little banner.

CAKE BANNER

WHAT YOU'LL NEED

cardstock
8-inch (20 cm) piece of string
assorted washi tape
lollipop sticks, straws,
   or skewers

1. Cut cardstock into ½-inch by 3-inch (1.2 cm by 7.5 cm) strips.

2. Place string on your workspace. Place the cardstock strips on the string so that the short end of each strip rests against the string.

3. One strip at a time, fold washi tape over the string and cardstock.

4. Trim the tape into flag shapes and discard any excess tape and cardstock.

5. String your DIY washi bunting between two lollipop sticks or straws and stick onto the top of your cake or cupcake.

SUN TEA JARS

Pretty and sweet, these drinks are a decoration and a treat.

You can use the decorated jars for other beverages, too—think flavored milks or fruit juice for brunch—but don't leave those drinks in the sun. Just keep them in the fridge.

WHAT YOU'LL NEED

fresh fruit
tea bags
cold water
mason jars and lids
fabric
glue
ribbons
straws
adhesive letters

1. Wash your jars before beginning.

2. Place fabric right side down on your work surface. Trace your jar's lid on it, and then draw another circle 1.5 inches (4 cm) larger on all sides.

3. Cut out the larger circle of fabric. Then make small cuts from the outer circle to the smaller circle.

4. Coat the lid with glue. Place fabric on the lid, right side out, and press it down smooth, removing all air bubbles. Pull the fabric over the sides and under the lid, wrapping them inside the lip of the lid. Cut off any extra fabric.

5. Use a ribbon to tie a straw to each jar. Add an adhesive letter to personalize each drink.

6. Fill jars with fresh fruit (such as citrus fruits, berries, or stone fruits like peaches or nectarines), a teabag (any flavor you like!) and fresh, cold water.

7. Serve tea with ice when you're ready to refresh your guests.

A delicious treat in her own personalized mug. Make these ahead of time for a sweet surprise.

HAND-PAINTED MUGS & PINK VELVET HOT CHOCOLATE

Try personalizing each mug with a friend's name, or using the same few colors so that each mug coordinates with the others.

The design on these mugs will stand up to hand washing, but it may start to come off in the dishwasher.

WHAT YOU'LL NEED

white mugs
rubbing alcohol
oil-based markers
2 tablespoons (30 grams)
   unsweetened cocoa
1 tablespoon (15 grams)
   chocolate chips
2 tablespoons (30 grams) sugar
¼ cup (59 ml) water
2 cups (500 ml) milk
¼ teaspoon (1 ml) vanilla
pink food coloring

1 Wipe down the mug with rubbing alcohol.

2 Draw your design on your mug.

3 Place your mug(s) on a cookie sheet and place in a cold oven.

4 Allow to preheat to 350 degrees F (180 degrees C) and bake for a total of thirty minutes.

5 Cool in the oven, and make sure you let the mugs cool thoroughly before touching them—they'll be hot for a few hours. Wash your mugs before using for Pink Velvet Hot Chocolate:

6 Combine cocoa, chocolate chips, sugar, and water in a mug. Microwave for thirty seconds, then stir. Microwave for another thirty seconds, or until the chocolate chips are completely melted. Stir everything well.

7 Slowly add milk and vanilla. Stir, and heat for one to two minutes, or until hot. Stir in food coloring.

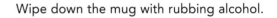

SALADS ON A STICK

WHAT YOU'LL NEED

your favorite vegetables
and fruits, cut in bite-size pieces
cheese cubes
wooden skewers

Keep your hands clean for crafting by making easy-to-eat salads on sticks. Just slide bite-size vegetables and cheese cubes onto wood skewers.

Try some of these combinations:

Wedge: iceburg lettuce, bacon, and grape tomato drizzled with ranch dressing and bleu cheese crumbles

Greek: grape tomatoes, feta cheese, cucumbers, black olives, and red onions, drizzled with Greek salad dressing

Sweet Strawberry: strawberries, spinach, and mandarin oranges drizzled with poppyseed dressing

Chef: romaine lettuce, hard-boiled eggs, ham, cucumber, and bread cubes, drizzled with your favorite dressing and shredded cheese

Plain skewers are so boring!
Use one of these ideas to dress them up:
* fold washi or glitter tape over the sticks and trim to make pennant or flag shapes
* cut sticky-back craft foam into shapes, such as circles or stars. Stick two shapes together with the skewer in the middle
* tie ribbon or fabric scraps to the sticks

RAINBOW FRUIT IN GLITTER CUPS

Glitter makes everything great! Dress up plain fruit with glamorous accessories.

UTENSILS

1 Paint the silverware handles with decoupage glue. Dip the wet handles directly into glitter. Tap off excess glitter, and let the glue dry for at least half an hour.

2 Add another layer of decoupage glue, sprinkling on addional glitter in any bare areas. Let the glue dry completely before using.

CUPS

1 Paint the bottom third of the cups with decoupage glue. Sprinkle on glitter, with a heavier layer near the bottom and a lighter layer farther up the cup. Tap off excess. Let the glue dry for at least half an hour. Then cover any glittered areas with another layer of decoupage glue.

FRUIT

Layer fruits by color for a healthful, rainbowy snack.

Red: strawberries, cherries, watermelon, pomegranate seeds, raspberries, red apples

Orange: oranges, mandarin oranges, mango, canteloupe, peaches, nectarines, papaya, apricots, grapefruit

Yellow: pineapple, yellow watermelon, bananas, yellow apples

Green: honeydew melon, green grapes, kiwi, pears, green apples

Blue: blackberries, blueberries, currants

Purple: purple grapes, plums, dried cranberries, figs

Serve with a dollop of whipped cream and a sprig of mint.

SWEET SNACK

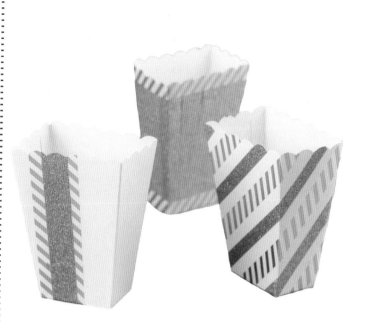

WHAT YOU'LL NEED

5 cups (about 85 grams) popped
  popcorn
1 cup (about 100 grams) pretzels
¼ cup (about 25 grams) mini
  marshmallows
¼ cup (about 25 grams) each of pink
  candy melts, chocolate candies, pastel
  sprinkles, and purple candy melts
½ cup (about 50 grams) pastel
  chocolate candies

1. Spread popcorn, pretzels, and marshmallows onto a baking sheet lined with parchment paper.

2. Place one color candy melts in a sandwich bag. Melt in a microwave at 50% power for one minute. Squeeze bag to stir candy melts. Melt for another thirty seconds or until candy is completely melted.

3. Snip the end off the sandwich bag and drizzle candy melts over the popcorn and marshmallows.

4. Sprinkle a third of the chocolate candies and sprinkles over the drizzled candy melts.

5. Repeat steps 2-4 with the other candy melts.

6. Place the baking sheet in a freezer for five minutes or until chocolate is hardened.

Cover popcorn boxes—available at grocery and craft stores—with glittery washi tape in different patterns.

You can fill these boxes with any munchable you and your friends love!

Lazy Crafternoon and Craft It Yourself are published by
Capstone Young Readers
1710 Roe Crest Drive
North Mankato, Minnesota 56003
www.mycapstone.com

Library of Congress Cataloging-in-Publication Data is available on the
Library of Congress website.

ISBN: 978-1-62370-751-4

Summary: Use this craft book to spend a lazy crafternoon making
projects with your friends.

Designer: Lori Bye
Creative Director: Heather Kindseth
Photos: Karon Dubke/Capstone Studio

Projects crafted by Lori Blackwell, Mari Bolte, Lori Bye,
Sarah Holden, Heather Kindseth, Marcy Morin, Sarah Schuette

Image credits: All photographs by Capstone Studio: Karon Dubke except: Shutterstock:
Africa Studio, 7 (bottom right), Ann Haritonenko, back cover (bottom right), 5 (top right), 7 (middle),
BhFoton, 16 (top right), Jenn Huls, 15, 83 (bottom right), Kaponia Aliaksei, 9 (bottom left),
MANDY GODBEHEAR, 7 (top), marilyn barbone, 25 (top), nenetus, 5 (top left), Picsfive,
cover (top right), Pressmaster, 5 (bottom), wavebreakmedia, back cover (bottom left) 7 (bottom left)

Design Elements: Shutterstock: ARaspopova, pixelliebe, Studio Lulu, Tossaporn Sakkabanchom

Special thanks to Dede Barton, Shelly Lyons, and Mari Bolte

Printed and bound in China.
009597F16